MARS LANDERS

BY
JOHN HAMILTON

Abdo & Daughters
An imprint of Abdo Publishing | abdopublishing.com

abdopublishing.com

Published by Abdo Publishing, a division of ABDO, PO Box 398166, Minneapolis, Minnesota 55439. Copyright © 2019 by Abdo Consulting Group, Inc. International copyrights reserved in all countries. No part of this book may be reproduced in any form without written permission from the publisher. Abdo & Daughters™ is a trademark and logo of Abdo Publishing.

Printed in the United States of America, North Mankato, Minnesota.
052018
092018

Editor: Sue Hamilton
Copy Editor: Bridget O'Brien
Graphic Design: Sue Hamilton
Cover Design: Candice Keimig and Pakou Moua
Cover Photo: iStock
Interior Images: All Images NASA, except: European Space Agency-pgs 4-5, 32, 33, 39 & 45; Granger Historical Picture Archive-pgs 13 & 44; Roscosmos-pg 26; Shutterstock-pgs 10-11 & 12; Wikimedia/Jeff Kubina-pg 24.

Library of Congress Control Number: 2017963902
Publisher's Cataloging-in-Publication Data
Names: Hamilton, John, author.
Title: Mars landers / by John Hamilton
Description: Minneapolis, Minnesota : Abdo Publishing, 2019. | Series: Mission to Mars | Includes online resources and index.
Identifiers: ISBN 9781532115936 (lib.bdg.) | ISBN 9781532156861 (ebook)
Subjects: LCSH: Space vehicles--Landing--Mars (Planet)--Juvenile literature. | Mars (Planet)--Aeronautics--Juvenile literature. | Mars (Planet)--Exploration--Equipment and supplies--Juvenile literature. | Mars (Planet)--Exploration--Juvenile literature.
Classification: DDC 523.43--dc23

CONTENTS

LANDING ON MARS

Starting in the mid-1970s and continuing to the present day, spacecraft from Earth have been landing on the mysterious planet Mars. They have included the groundbreaking Viking landers of the 1970s and the more recent Phoenix polar lander and the planned InSight probe.

To get to the planet's surface, landers must overcome great odds. They travel millions of miles through deep space, arriving at Mars with pinpoint accuracy. They drop through Mars's thin atmosphere at hyper speeds that can cause delicate electronics to burn up or shake apart. They slow down with perfectly timed rockets and parachutes to avoid crashing on the rocky ground.

These engineering marvels land automatically. Mars is so far from Earth that human controllers can't save the landers if something goes wrong. Radio signals take too long to communicate with spacecraft in real-time.

Landers are sent on this perilous journey so we can unlock the secrets of Mars's harsh landscape. The mysteries we solve on Mars may one day help us understand Earth's own history and future.

A lander fires its retrorockets on its descent to the Martian surface.

WHY GO TO MARS?

Before scientists knew how to build landers that could set down on Mars, orbiters blazed a trail to the Red Planet. In late 1971,

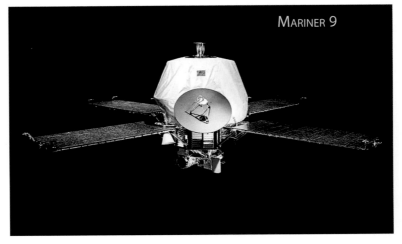

MARINER 9

Mariner 9 arrived at Mars on November 14, 1971.

NASA's Mariner 9 began a nearly yearlong investigation of Mars. The 1,245-pound (565-kg) probe was the first spacecraft to orbit another planet besides Earth. At the closest point in its orbit, it came within 1,025 miles (1,650 km) of the Martian surface.

Mariner 9 took thousands of images and beamed them back to Earth by radio. Scientists who studied the 7,329 images were astonished. Earlier Mariner probes had hinted at a dead, crater-filled planet. But Mars held many surprises.

The photos from Mariner 9 revealed that Mars has huge volcanoes rising above its northern plains. The biggest, Olympus Mons, is 100 times the size of Hawaii's Mauna Kea. It is by far the largest volcano in the solar system. Mars also has a canyon nearly 2,485 miles (4,000 km) long and several miles deep, dwarfing Arizona's Grand Canyon. (The Martian canyon was named Valles Marineris in honor of Mariner 9.)

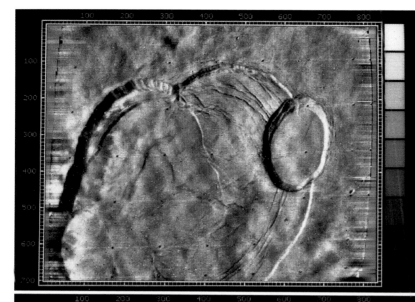

Mariner 9 image of the central caldera of the Martian volcano, Olympus Mons.

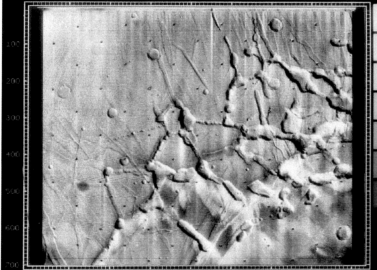

Mariner 9 view of the "labyrinth" at the western end of Vallis Marineris.

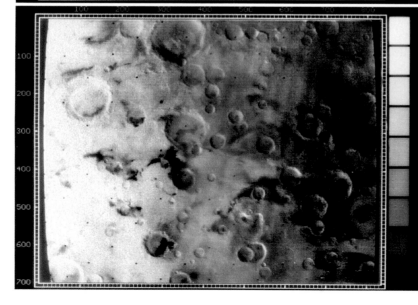

Mariner 9 image of Promethei Sinus near Mars' south pole. The area is filled with large craters.

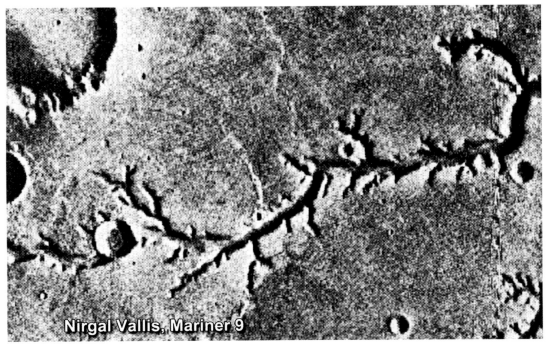
Nirgal Vallis, Mariner 9

This view of channels on Mars came from NASA's Mariner 9 orbiter. What created these channels? Could water have flowed on Mars long ago? Scientists wanted to know more about the Red Planet's history. To get this information, they needed a craft to land on the planet.

Most exciting of all was the hint of water on the Martian surface. Photos from Mariner 9 clearly showed ancient, dry riverbeds that must have flowed with water long ago. Scientists also began to suspect that the planet's north polar ice cap contained not just frozen carbon dioxide (dry ice) as first thought, but also huge amounts of frozen water.

The chance that Mars once contained vast amounts of water was a very exciting idea. Water is one of the key ingredients of life as we know it. Did life also evolve on Mars? And if water could be found on Mars today, maybe buried underground, perhaps life still thrived on the Red Planet.

However, in 1971 there was no way to tell for sure if Mars harbored life by looking down from an orbiter hundreds of miles above. Science experiments had to be conducted on the surface. Even as Mariner 9 continued to map Mars, scientists in the United States began designing a new kind of spacecraft that could land safely on the planet. These new probes were called landers. In the coming years, they would tell us more about the mysterious Red Planet than ever before.

A technician checks the Viking lander's soil sampler in May 1971. The lander's creation depended on the experience gained from previous NASA projects, including the Ranger, Surveyor, and Apollo programs.

MARS 2 & 3

Starting in the mid-1950s, the United States and the former Soviet Union (much of which is today's Russia) were locked in the Space Race. They competed to be the first in many areas of space exploration.

In 1970, the Soviet Union's Venera 7 touched down on the planet Venus. It was the first spacecraft to land successfully on an alien world. Unfortunately, it landed too hard. Damage from the landing and the planet's high temperatures caused the probe to fail. It sent radio signals back to Earth for less than an hour.

The Soviet Union's Mars program was just as ambitious. Sputnik 24 was built to land on the Martian surface. It launched in 1962, but the spacecraft failed to leave Earth orbit. Then, at the end of 1971, a pair of Soviet spacecraft safely arrived at Mars. They were called Mars 2 and Mars 3. Unlike the American Mariner 9 probe, the Soviet spacecraft included landers. They were big machines. Each weighed about 2,700 pounds (1,225 kg) with fuel.

After entering the Martian atmosphere, the spherically shaped landers were designed to fire braking rockets and use parachutes to slow down. Once safely on the surface, four pedals would unfold to make sure the landers were upright. Next, science experiments would be performed on the Martian soil and weather, and would be radioed back to Earth.

The landers also included shoebox-sized rovers that could explore the Martian surface. The rovers used metal skis that lifted and pushed them across the ground. They could also detect and avoid obstacles.

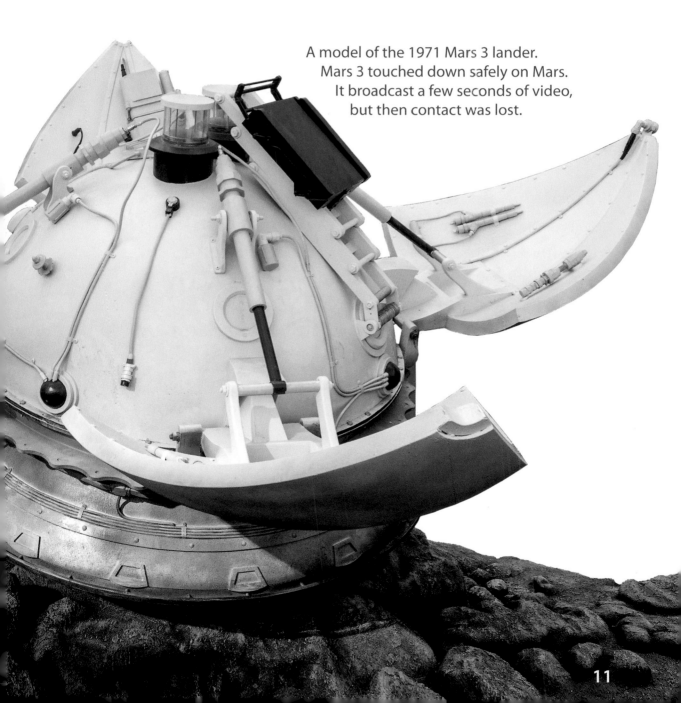

A model of the 1971 Mars 3 lander. Mars 3 touched down safely on Mars. It broadcast a few seconds of video, but then contact was lost.

A postage stamp shows the soft landing planned for Mars 3. It did land safely on December 2, 1971. However, its transmissions from the Martian surface lasted only a few seconds before contact was lost.

Mars 2 and Mars 3 were very advanced machines for their time. However, limited technology and faulty design left no room for error. Although the Soviet orbiters had some success, bad luck struck the landers. Both were doomed.

On November 27, 1971, the Mars 2 lander plunged toward the planet at high speed. Its parachute failed to open, and Mars 2 was destroyed on impact. Although it crashed, it became the first human object to reach Mars.

Unlike its twin, Mars 3 landed safely on December 2, 1971. For several seconds, it sent a partial television image of the Martian surface. Then, all contact was lost. A planet-wide dust storm may have harmed the probe's delicate electronics, but we'll probably never know for sure what happened.

Both Soviet landers could have made breakthroughs in science. Instead, the world would have to wait for America's turn. Five years later the history-making Viking landers would be ready to explore Mars.

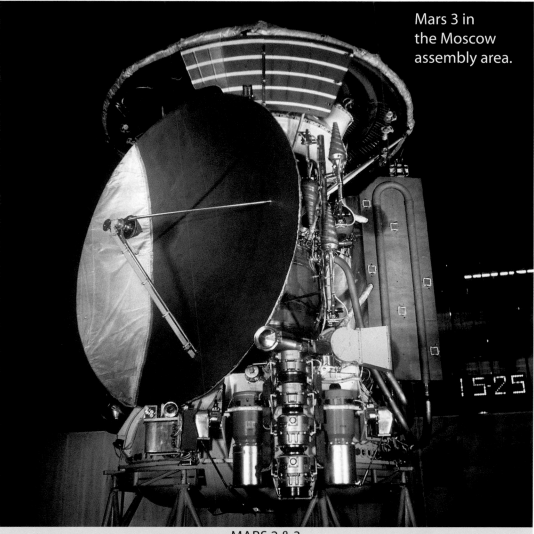

Mars 3 in the Moscow assembly area.

MARS 2 & 3

Mission: Mars orbiter/lander

Launch: Mars 2: May 19, 1971
Mars 3: May 28, 1971

Launch Vehicle: Proton K/Blok D

Mars Arrival: Mars 2: November 27, 1971
Mars 3: December 2, 1971

Mission End: August 22, 1972

Spacecraft weight (mass): 10,250 pounds (4,649 kg)

THE VIKING LANDERS

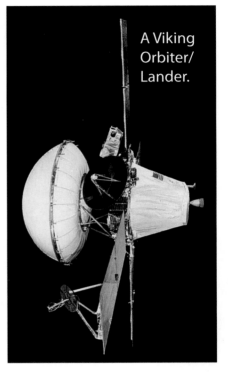

A Viking Orbiter/ Lander.

In March 1974, two more landers from the Soviet Union tried to beat the United States to the Red Planet. However, bad luck continued to plague the Soviet space program. The Mars 6 lander crashed on the surface, while the Mars 7 spacecraft missed the planet completely. The stage was set for the Americans.

In 1976, twin spacecraft from the United States entered orbit around Mars. They were the Viking 1 and Viking 2 probes that NASA had launched in late 1975. After nearly a year of traveling through deep space, each Viking reached the Red Planet with pinpoint accuracy.

Each spacecraft included two parts. The orbiters were designed to take high-resolution color images from high above the planet. The stars of the mission, however, were the landers. They would conduct experiments on the Martian soil, including searching for signs of life. Viking 1 and Viking 2 were the most ambitious spacecraft ever to explore Mars at that time.

In 1971, the NASA Mariner 9 orbiter proved that water flowed on Mars long ago. Water is a necessary ingredient for life as we know it. Could life have sprung from the Red Planet, as it had on Earth? The scientists who built the Viking landers were determined to find out.

Mission: Mars orbiter/lander

Launch: Viking 1: August 20, 1975
              Viking 2: September 9, 1975

Launch Vehicle: Titan III/Centaur

Mars Arrival: Viking 1: June 19, 1976
              Viking 2: August 7, 1976

Touchdown:
    Viking 1 lander: July 20, 1976
    Viking 2 lander: Sept. 3, 1976

Mission End:
    Viking 1 lander: Nov. 13, 1982
    Viking 2 lander: April 11, 1980

Spacecraft weight (mass),
  lander only: 1,262 pounds (572 kg)

The Viking landers were marvels of engineering for their time. About the size of a small SUV (sport utility vehicle), they were made of aluminum and titanium alloys. Each weighed about 1,262 pounds (572 kg). They included scientific instruments, communications gear, and cameras. Landing rockets were mounted underneath.

Each lander contained a miniature biological laboratory to search for microscopic Martian life. Also on board were instruments to measure the Martian weather, plus a seismometer to detect possible marsquakes. Controlling all the equipment were twin onboard computers.

The landers were sterilized before launching. The search for life on Mars would be ruined if the landers detected Earth-born bacteria that had mistakenly hitchhiked a ride. To prevent this, the Viking landers were baked at 234 degrees Fahrenheit (112° C) for 40 hours. Then they were sealed in a protective shell to keep them germ free. Next, the spacecraft were mounted atop rockets, ready for liftoff.

NASA's clean-room technicians prepare a Viking lander for sterilization. The process is called dry heat microbial reduction.

Viking 2 launched from Florida's Cape Canaveral on September 9, 1975. The spacecraft followed its twin, Viking 1. Both arrived at Mars just weeks apart.

On August 20, 1975, a powerful Titan III/Centaur rocket blasted off from Florida's Cape Canaveral. The launch went smoothly, sending the Viking 1 orbiter/lander on its yearlong journey to Mars. Less than three weeks later, on September 9, 1975, Viking 2 followed its twin toward the Red Planet. The landers piggybacked on the orbiters all the way to Mars. Once they reached orbit, they separated and began their decent to the Martian surface.

The Viking 1 lander is assembled at Martin Marietta Aerospace. The probe had to carry out its landing without any help from controllers on Earth.

One of the biggest challenges in designing an unmanned lander is controlling it. In 1969, the Apollo 11 lunar module *Eagle* nearly crashed into a boulder field during its descent to the Moon. Astronauts Neil Armstrong and Edwin "Buzz" Aldrin took control of the spacecraft and steered it away from danger. With Martian probes, there are no astronauts to take over if something goes wrong.

Another problem with interplanetary probes is the vast distance of space. At their closest, Mars and Earth are usually about 35 million miles (56 million km) apart. The Viking radio signals, traveling at the speed of light, would take about 3 minutes to reach Earth. It would then take another 3 minutes for NASA to send a signal back to Mars. (Radio signals from the Moon take just one second.) Earth and Mars would be even farther apart when the Vikings were scheduled to land. If something went wrong on Mars, the crisis would be over long before engineers at NASA could do anything about it. Each Viking lander had to carry out its landing without any help from controllers on Earth.

Another problem with landing a spacecraft is slowing down enough to avoid crashing. At first, each Viking craft would use Mars's own atmosphere to slow down. Even though the air on Mars is very thin, spacecraft can use a technique called "aerobraking." This uses the friction of moving through the air at high speed to slow down. However, the friction generates a lot of heat. To avoid damage, the landers and their delicate electronics were protected by saucer-shaped heat shields.

NASA scientists at the Langley Research Center in Virginia stand in front of the aeroshell that protected the Viking 1 lander during its entry into the Martian atmosphere in 1976. An aeroshell is made of a heat shield and a backshell that contains parachutes and other items used for entry.

TOUCHDOWN!

On July 20, 1976, the Viking 1 lander separated from the orbiter and began its descent. (It was the seven-year anniversary of the Apollo 11 Moon landing.) Cameras aboard the Viking orbiters helped

Viking 1 and 2 used aerobraking, parachutes, and retrorockets to safely land on Mars.

scientists pick the safest place to land, in a part of Mars called Chryse Planitia. Anxious scientists on Earth held their breath as the lander began its long, arching fall to the Martian surface.

The lander sped through the upper atmosphere at more than 10,000 miles per hour (16,093 kph). That is about 4 times the speed of a bullet. Aerobraking slowed the spacecraft down. Friction caused the outer surface of the heat shield to reach a scorching 2,700 degrees Fahrenheit (1,482° C). The lander remained safe inside.

By the time the lander was 3.7 miles (6 km) above the surface, it had slowed down to about 600 miles per hour (966 kph). A billowing, 52-foot (16-m) cloth parachute was shot out of a small cannon. Explosive bolts jettisoned what was left of the charred heat shield. Viking 1's three landing legs unfolded. They were spring-loaded to cushion the impact of landing.

The massive parachute helped slow down Viking 1 to just over 134 miles per hour (216 kph). That was still too fast. About .9 mile (1.5 km) above the surface, the parachute detached. Three radar-controlled retrorockets ignited under the lander, slowing it even more.

At 8:12 a.m. Eastern Daylight Time, the Viking 1 lander gently touched down on Mars after a journey of 440 million miles (708 million km). It impacted the surface at about 5.4 miles per hour (8.7 kph). That's about the same force as jumping off a tall kitchen stool.

Viking 1's engines shut down, and silence returned to the Martian surface. For 19 long minutes, NASA controllers on Earth could only sit and wait for a signal from Viking 1. Was the lander safe, or had it crashed? Then word raced through Mission Control: "Touchdown! We have touchdown!"

During the final landing stage, Viking 1 and 2 used retrorockets to slow their descent to the Martian surface. A parachute carried away the protective aeroshell.

The first clear photo from the surface of Mars was taken just minutes after the Viking 1 lander set down on the Red Planet. One of the lander's footpads is seen in the lower right corner. NASA scientists took this photo first so they could see how the footpad would affect the Martian soil.

Shortly after landing, Viking 1 switched on its twin cameras. The first image it sent back to Earth was a black-and-white picture that showed one of Viking 1's landing pads resting in the rocky soil. Later, color images revealed a flat, reddish Martian landscape with a salmon-pink sky. (Small dust particles in the air give Mars its pinkish-colored sky.)

Less than seven weeks after Viking 1's success, it was joined by Viking 2. On September 3, 1976, the lander touched down safely at Mars's Utopia Planitia, about 4,000 miles (6,437 km) west of Viking 1.

The surface of each landing site was strewn with rocks and boulders in various shapes and sizes. The landscape resembled the deserts of the American Southwest. An orange-colored, sandy soil covered the ground. It lay in drifts, thanks to the Martian breezes.

Later, the Viking landers chemically analyzed the soil. It was like a loosely packed iron-rich clay. It was reddish because of a chemical reaction with the iron called oxidation—rust.

When Viking 1's first day came to an end, it issued the first weather report from Mars: "Light winds from the east in the late afternoon… Maximum wind, 15 miles per hour (24 kph). Temperature ranging from -122 degrees Fahrenheit (-86° C) just after dawn to -22 degrees Fahrenheit (-30° C)."

The Viking landers took the first close-up photographs of Mars. The high-resolution images were in black-and-white and in color. In total, the landers sent back more than 4,500 images of the Martian surface, delighting scientists, and everyone else, on Earth.

The Viking 1 lander took the first color image of Mars on July 21, 1976.

Each Viking lander included three biology laboratories. A 6-foot (1.8-m) -long robotic arm scooped up soil samples and delivered them to the labs. Several tests were designed to look for signs of life. For example, Earth plants "eat" carbon dioxide gas, and this can be measured. Other tests looked for tiny organisms in the Martian soil.

A close-up view of a Viking lander's robotic arm.

At first, the Viking tests for life were promising. But when the data was examined further, most scientists believed that no Martian life was detected. Many scientists think the only way to tell for sure is to bring a soil sample back to Earth for further study—or send human astronauts to Mars.

The Viking 2 lander's surface sampler arm carefully digs between rocks to obtain Martian soil for analysis.

Viking 2 takes a "selfie" with the rocky field of Mars's Utopia Planitia behind it. The lander's American flag decal is seen clearly in the image.

The Viking landers were meant to last about 90 days on the surface of Mars. They actually lasted for several years, working far beyond their mission. The Viking 2 lander finally stopped sending signals to Earth on April 11, 1980. The Viking 1 lander stopped working on November 13, 1982.

A lot of the technology used on later Mars missions was pioneered by the Viking landers. Many questions remain, but the science they performed on the planet was a big step forward in learning about the Red Planet.

MARS PATHFINDER

After the successful American Viking landers, the Soviet Union continued its own efforts to send spacecraft to Mars. In 1988, they launched Phobos 1 and Phobos 2. The probes were sent to study Mars and its two moons, Phobos and Deimos. They were also designed to drop landers on Phobos to examine the moon up close. Unfortunately, Phobos 1's computer shut down the probe's systems while it was between Earth and Mars. Phobos 2 suffered a similar fate. Its computer failed just before the lander was ready to be dropped onto the Martian moon.

In 1991, most of the Soviet Union became the Russian Federation. The Russian space program tried again to reach Mars in 1996. Sadly, they were met with another failure. The Mars 96 orbiter/lander spacecraft crashed into the Pacific Ocean shortly after launch.

The Soviet Union sent Phobos 1 and Phobos 2 to study Mars in 1988. However, neither craft succeeded in their mission.

In 1997, the United States finally returned to Mars. More than 20 years had passed since the Viking missions. This time, NASA sent a spacecraft called Mars Pathfinder. Piggybacking on the lander was a microwave-oven sized rover called Sojourner. (The rover was named after U.S. Civil War abolitionist Sojourner Truth. The word sojourner means "traveler.")

Pathfinder was part of NASA's Discovery Program. Its motto was "better, faster, cheaper." Each mission was designed to be built quickly and for relatively little money (for a spacecraft). Pathfinder's simple mission: test the Sojourner rover in the hostile environment of Mars. The Pathfinder lander itself would take pictures and perform science experiments.

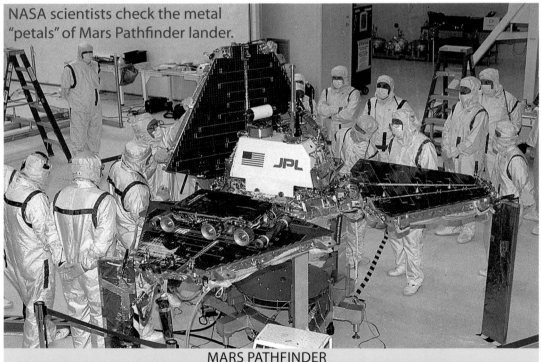

NASA scientists check the metal "petals" of Mars Pathfinder lander.

MARS PATHFINDER			
Mission:	Mars lander/rover	Mars Touchdown:	July 4, 1997
Launch:	December 4, 1996	Mission End:	September 27, 1997
Launch Vehicle:	Delta II	Spacecraft weight (mass):	1,020 pounds (463 kg)

A panorama photo taken by Mars Pathfinder.

Mars Pathfinder lifted off from Florida's Cape Canaveral on December 4, 1996. It began a long, arching path through space. By the time it caught up with Mars in July 1997, it had travelled more than 300 million miles (483 million km).

On July 4, 1997, Pathfinder landed on the rocky Ares Vallis plain of Mars. A large parachute helped slow it down through the atmosphere. A unique system of oversized airbags cushioned the final impact. Pathfinder survived the landing in great shape, and soon began its work.

Even though the Sojourner rover was the star of the mission, the Pathfinder lander flawlessly performed its own science experiments. It monitored the Martian weather, including temperature, wind speed, and atmospheric pressure. The first night on Ares Vallis, the temperature dropped to a bone-chilling -64 degrees Fahrenheit (-53° C).

The Mars Pathfinder lander was also equipped with a stereoscopic camera. It was mounted on a pop-up mast that boosted the camera several feet above the ground. The camera took more than 16,500 high-resolution images of the surrounding Martian landscape. The photos were in black-and-white, color, and in 3-D.

The Pathfinder lander lasted many weeks beyond its expected lifespan of 30 days. Finally, on September 27, 1997, the lander lost contact with Earth after nearly three months. The harsh conditions on Mars, especially the cold, probably caused its computer or batteries to fail.

The Pathfinder lander was officially renamed the Carl Sagan Memorial Station. Carl Sagan was a popular astronomer who had died earlier in 1997. His work greatly helped in the exploration of Mars.

MARS POLAR LANDER

S cientists who work on sending spaceships to Mars know that it is hard to do. So many things can go wrong, from launch explosions to crashing while trying to land, and everything in between. The success of the Mars Pathfinder mission gave NASA managers confidence that Mars missions really could be achieved quickly and cheaply.

The Mars Polar Lander was a 640-pound (290-kg) spacecraft. Its main mission was to search for water ice near the Martian south pole. It carried two robotic bullets that would be fired into the ground just before the probe landed. They would burrow deeply into the soil, where the harmful effect of the Sun's rays had not altered the dirt's chemistry. That information could tell scientists much about the early geology of Mars.

Technicians inspect the Mars Polar Lander.

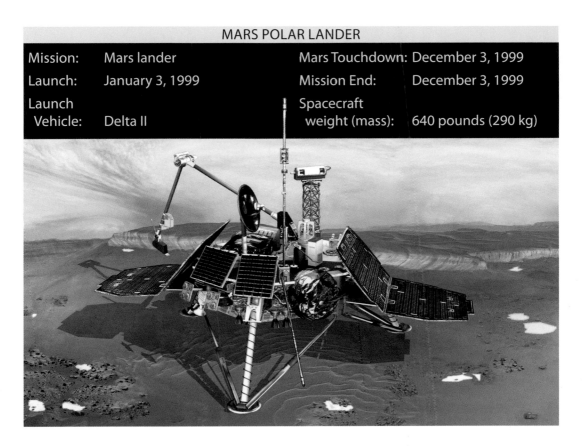

MARS POLAR LANDER			
Mission:	Mars lander	Mars Touchdown:	December 3, 1999
Launch:	January 3, 1999	Mission End:	December 3, 1999
Launch Vehicle:	Delta II	Spacecraft weight (mass):	640 pounds (290 kg)

Mars Polar Lander was launched on January 3, 1999. It reached Mars on December 3, 1999. It was aiming for a region called Planum Australe. Everything seemed to be going well as the spacecraft entered the planet's thin atmosphere and streaked toward the ground. Suddenly, contact with the spacecraft was lost. Many minutes passed with no signal from the lander. Finally, Mars Polar Lander was declared lost.

A team of scientists later discovered that as the probe approached the surface, its landing legs extended as planned. However, the vibrations caused the on-board computer to think it had already landed. It shut down the retrorockets too soon. The lander fell the last 100 feet (30 m) to the frozen ground and was destroyed. The Mars Polar Lander was an embarrassing failure.

BEAGLE 2

The next lander to explore Mars did not come from the United States or Russia. Instead, it came from Europe. The European Space Agency (ESA) has been building and flying spacecraft and equipment since the late 1970s. Its members represent 22 European countries, including France, the United Kingdom, Germany, and Italy.

The Beagle 2 lander was built by scientists from the United Kingdom. Its mission was to search for signs of life in the soil. It had tools that could scoop up and analyze soil and rocks with a robotic arm.

Beagle 2 piggybacked to Mars aboard the Mars Express orbiter. It was the ESA's first try at visiting another planet. Mars Express launched on June 2, 2003. Although the orbiter was very successful, Beagle 2 met with disaster.

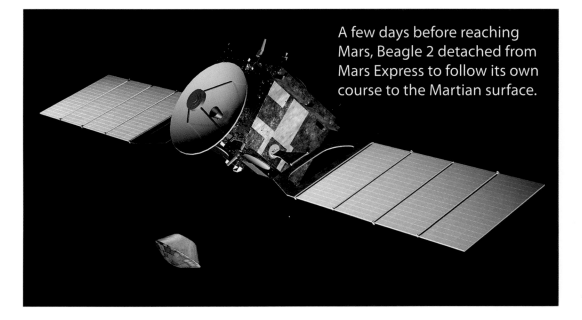

A few days before reaching Mars, Beagle 2 detached from Mars Express to follow its own course to the Martian surface.

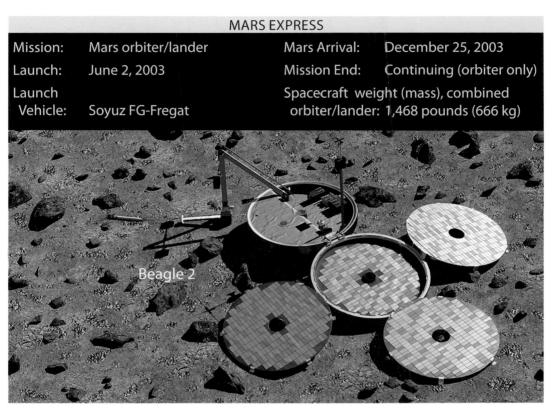

MARS EXPRESS			
Mission:	Mars orbiter/lander	Mars Arrival:	December 25, 2003
Launch:	June 2, 2003	Mission End:	Continuing (orbiter only)
Launch Vehicle:	Soyuz FG-Fregat	Spacecraft weight (mass), combined orbiter/lander: 1,468 pounds (666 kg)	

Beagle 2

Shaped like a large bowl, the Beagle 2 lander weighed about 73 pounds (33 kg) and measured 3.3 feet (1 m) in diameter. It had four solar panels it used for power. A few days before Mars Express reached Mars, Beagle 2 detached and followed its own course. On December 25, 2003, it began its descent to the Martian surface. It used parachutes to slow its speed, and airbags to cushion the impact with the ground. However, attempts to contact the spacecraft after landing were met with silence. The mission had failed.

Later, images from NASA orbiters revealed Beagle 2. Its solar panels had not unfolded properly after landing. The radio transmitter was blocked, and it could not produce the power it needed. Beagle 2 could not call home for help, and it soon met an untimely end.

PHOENIX MARS LANDER

n 2002, NASA's Mars Odyssey orbiter discovered that the north polar region of Mars had huge amounts of water ice buried under the surface. NASA decided to try a second time to land a spacecraft near a Martian pole. Mars Polar Lander had failed in 1999 at the south pole. This time, a NASA spacecraft would land on the opposite side of the planet. Its name was Phoenix Mars Lander. (Phoenix is the bird of ancient myths that was reborn from fire.) The new spacecraft's design would be based on the earlier lander, but with many improvements.

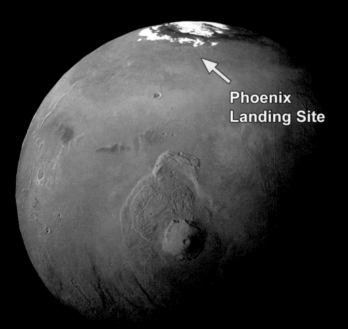

Phoenix
Landing Site

PHOENIX MARS LANDER

PHOENIX MARS LANDER			
Mission:	Mars lander	Mars Touchdown:	May 25, 2008
Launch:	August 4, 2007	Mission End:	November 2, 2008
Launch Vehicle:	Delta II	Spacecraft weight (mass):	770 pounds (349 kg)

The Phoenix lander had two mission goals. The first was to study the history of Martian water. To do this, it would analyze samples of the arctic ice. Water is a necessary ingredient for life. The lander's second goal was to study whether the Martian arctic soil could support life. By digging deep into the ground, perhaps the lander could detect bacteria lying dormant in the dry, bitterly cold Martian environment.

Phoenix was equipped with a long robot arm. It was designed to dig deeply into the soil and then bring samples to be studied by instruments on the lander. A camera was mounted on the scoop end of the robotic arm. Phoenix was also equipped with microscopes, gas analyzers, instruments for studying the Martian weather, and a high-resolution stereo camera mounted on a tall mast rising above the lander.

Phoenix Mars Lander blasted off from Florida's Cape Canaveral on August 4, 2007. Its journey to Mars went smoothly, and it arrived on May 25, 2008. As the probe descended to the surface, it used a parachute to slow its speed. From high above, NASA's Mars Reconnaissance Orbiter captured an image of Phoenix with its parachute deployed.

During the last landing stage, Phoenix released its parachute and fired retrorockets. It touched down safely near the north pole in the Vastitas Borealis region. It was the site of a large ocean billions of years ago. Phoenix became the first lander to successfully land in a polar region of Mars.

Photos from Phoenix soon arrived at Mission Control on Earth. Unlike other landing sites, the photos revealed a very flat plain with few large rocks. Directly underneath the retrorockets were large white patches. These were areas swept clean of loose soil by the rockets, revealing hard layers of water ice. For the first time, a lander had made direct contact with water on Mars!

Phoenix landed on Mars using retrorockets. It became the first lander to successfully land in a polar region of the Red Planet.

Phoenix conducted science experiments for several months. It sent weather reports, dug for soil samples, and tested water ice. No microorganisms were found, but analysis of the ice revealed that flowing water was present near the poles in Mars's distant past.

Phoenix continued operating beyond its 90-day lifespan, but not for long. After 155 days on Mars, the lander fell silent. It became the victim of the coming winter at the north polar region, where temperatures had been falling to -142 degrees Fahrenheit (-97° C). Finally, the cold drained the lander's batteries faster than they could be recharged by the solar panels. NASA declared the mission over on November 2, 2008.

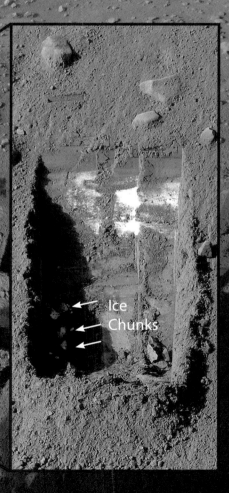

The Phoenix lander found water ice on Mars

Ice Chunks

SCHIAPARELLI EDM LANDER

In the early 2010s, the European Space Agency (ESA) teamed up with Roscosmos, the Russian space agency. They planned twin missions called ExoMars to look for past life on the Red Planet.

The first ExoMars mission contained two spacecraft. The ExoMars Trace Gas Orbiter was designed to look for small amounts of methane and other gasses in the Martian atmosphere. Scientists hoped to detect the by-product of life on the surface.

The other part of the mission was the Schiaparelli EDM lander. EDM stands for Entry, descent and landing Demonstrator Module. The spacecraft was named after the famous Italian astronomer Giovanni Schiaparelli. Schiaparelli EDM's goal was to test technology for future landing missions. It would also measure weather conditions, including electricity in the atmosphere. The spacecraft launched on March 14, 2016, and reached Mars in October 2016. (The second part of ExoMars, which includes a rover, will launch sometime in 2020.)

The Schiaparelli EDM lander separates from the ExoMars Trace Gas Orbiter.

EXOMARS			
Mission:	Mars orbiter/lander	Mars Arrival:	October 19, 2016
Launch:	March 14, 2016	Mission End:	Continuing (orbiter only)
Launch Vehicle:	Proton	Spacecraft weight (mass), combined orbiter/lander:	9,550 pounds (4,332 kg)

The ExoMars Trace Gas Orbiter successfully went into orbit around Mars and began its mission. Schiaparelli EDM, however, was not as lucky. On October 19, 2016, it entered the Martian atmosphere at 13,000 miles per hour (20,921 kph). It then began its descent to the Meridiani Planum region. A parachute and retrorockets helped slow it down. But instead of landing softly, the retrorockets shut down too soon. The spacecraft smashed into the ground at about 186 miles per hour (300 kph). It was totally destroyed.

Images later taken by NASA's Mars Reconnaissance Orbiter show the black scorch mark on the ground where Schiaparelli EDM crashed. Although the lander was lost, the mission was still a partial success. Unlike the earlier Beagle 2 lander, Schiaparelli EDM transmitted data to Earth as it fell. The landing system had been tested, and lessons were learned for future missions.

INSIGHT

One of the last areas of Mars to be explored is the planet's deep interior. How big is its core? What kinds of rocks are hidden deep below the surface, and is the hot core solid or molten? NASA's InSight lander will help scientists answer these questions. By studying Mars's crust, mantle, and core, we can learn a lot about how the inner solar system's rocky worlds were formed, including Earth.

NASA's InSight undergoes final preparations. InSight, short for Interior Exploration using Seismic Investigations, Geodesy, and Heat Transport, is the first mission dedicated to studying the deep interior of Mars. Its findings will advance understanding of the early history of all rocky planets, including Earth.

Seismometer

HP³

Heat Flow Probe

The InSight lander's three-legged design is based on NASA's Phoenix Mars Lander spacecraft. Additional science equipment was added. The most important tools will help InSight study the Martian interior. The first is a very sensitive seismometer that can measure marsquakes, as well as study the structure of Mars. It is so sensitive that it can even detect the vibrations made by meteorites striking other parts of the planet.

The second tool is called the Heat flow and Physical Properties Package (HP³). It measures the heat that rises from the planet's core. An 18-inch (46-cm) spike will burrow deep into the soil. It will use an internal hammering device to drive itself up to 16 feet (5 m) deep. A cable will trail the spike into the hole. It has heat sensors along its length. Scientists can measure the rate at which heat from the planet's interior reaches the sensors. From this data, they can learn about the structure of Mars's core.

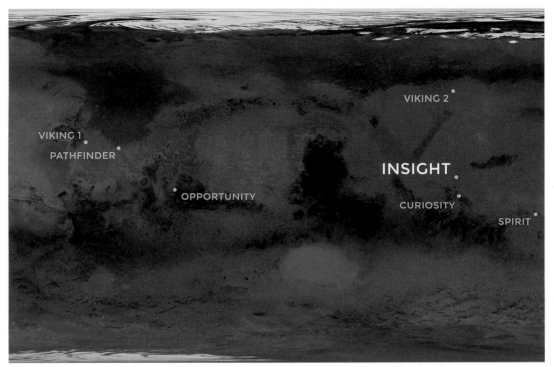

InSight's planned landing area is in the Elysium Planitia region, a flat, smooth plain just north of Mars's equator and near some major volcanoes. It is the perfect location for studying the deep interior of the Red Planet.

The InSight lander launched successfully on May 5, 2018, from California's Vandenberg Air Force Base. If all goes well, the spacecraft should arrive at Mars in late November 2018. It will have travelled about 301 million miles (484 million km) to Mars. It will enter the Martian atmosphere and attempt to land in the Elysium Planitia region, just south of an area containing major volcanoes.

Tagging along with InSight are two briefcase-sized spacecraft called CubeSats. They are equipped with radio antennas and solar panels for power. When the InSight lander descends to the surface, the mini-orbiters will relay information to scientists on Earth in just minutes.

A large parachute and retrorockets will slow InSight's descent. After landing softly with its three shock-absorbing legs, two solar panels will unfold to provide power to the lander. With solar panels extended, InSight is about the size of a large automobile.

If all goes according to plan, a 7.8-foot (2.4-m) robotic arm with cameras on its end will carefully place the seismometer and HP[3] heat flow experiments on the surface. The lander will also measure wind, temperature, and the local magnetic field.

If InSight completes its mission, scientists will have a much better understanding of Mars's deep interior, and how it formed. This data will also shed light on how all rocky planets form, including our home world of Earth.

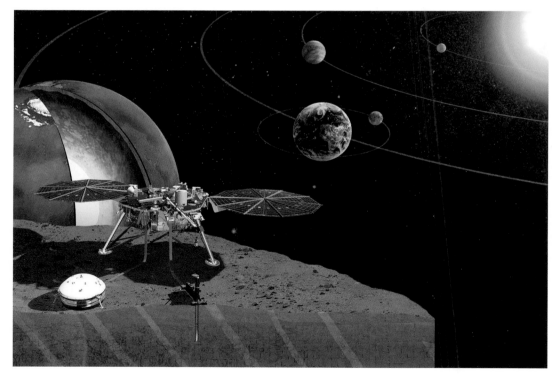

InSight's mission will lead to a better understanding of Mars's deep interior. This information will help us understand how all rocky planets form, including Earth.

TIMELINE

Mars 2 & 3

Nov. 27, 1971—Mars 2 (USSR) lander crashes, becoming the first human object to reach surface of planet.

Dec. 2, 1971—Mars 3 (USSR) orbiter arrives at Mars. Along with sister spacecraft Mars 2, automatically takes photos as featureless dust storm swirls on planet. Mars 3 lander touches down on surface but malfunctions after a few seconds.

Viking 1 & 2

July 20, 1976—Viking 1 (USA) lander is first spacecraft to safely touch down on the surface of Mars and complete its mission of photographing the landscape and analyzing soil samples.

Sept. 3, 1976—Viking 2 (USA) lander safely touches down on the surface of Mars.

Pathfinder & Sojourner

July 4, 1997—Mars Pathfinder (USA) safely lands. Monitors weather and takes high-resolution photos of surface. Accompanying Sojourner rover successfully deployed. Lander renamed Carl Sagan Memorial Station.

Mars Polar Lander

Dec. 3, 1999—Mars Polar Lander crashes on surface because retrorockets shut down too soon.

Mars Express

Dec. 25, 2003—The European Space Agency's Mars Express orbiter arrives at the Red Planet. Accompanying Beagle 2 lander begins its descent to the Martian surface. Attempts to contact the spacecraft after landing fail. Mars orbiter images later show that Beagle 2's solar panels fail to properly unfold. The Beagle 2 lander's mission fails, but Mars Express orbiter is successful.

Beagle 2

May 25, 2008—Phoenix Mars Lander (USA) safely touches down in Martian north polar region. First lander to make direct contact with water ice on Mars.

Phoenix Mars Lander

October 19, 2016—ExoMars Trace Gas Orbiter (joint European Space Agency and Roscosmos (Russia)) enters orbit around Mars.

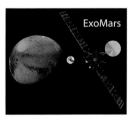
ExoMars

October 19, 2016—The ExoMars lander, Schiaparelli EDM (Entry, descent and landing Demonstrator Module), crashes into Mars. Retrorockets shut down too soon, causing spacecraft to hit surface at high speed, destroying it.

Schiaparelli EDM

May 5, 2018—InSight (USA) lander blasts off from Vandenberg Air Force Base, in California. Scheduled to land on Mars in late November 2018.

InSight

GLOSSARY

ABOLITIONIST

An activist who fought for freedom for slaves.

EUROPEAN SPACE AGENCY (ESA)

A space agency, like NASA, that builds and flies spacecraft that explore the solar system. Its headquarters is in Paris, France. As of 2018, there are 22 countries that are members of the ESA.

INTERPLANETARY

Located or traveling between the planets of a solar system.

METEORITE

A meteor that strikes the ground. A meteoroid is a solid object, usually rocky, that moves through space. It is much smaller than an asteroid, ranging from the size of a grain of sand to about one meter in diameter. If a meteoroid enters a planet's atmosphere, it becomes a meteor. Earth's atmosphere is so thick that most meteors burn up, becoming streaks in the sky, which we call "falling" or "shooting stars." If a meteor survives and strikes the ground, it is called a meteorite.

NATIONAL AERONAUTICS AND SPACE ADMINISTRATION (NASA)

A United States government space agency started in 1958. NASA's goals include space exploration, as well as increasing people's understanding of Earth, our solar system, and the universe.

ORBIT

The circular path a moon or spacecraft makes when traveling around a planet or other large celestial body. There are several satellites orbiting Mars, including NASA's Mars Reconnaissance Orbiter and the European Space Agency's ExoMars Trace Gas Orbiter.

PROBE

An unmanned space vehicle that is sent on missions that are too dangerous, or would take too long, for human astronauts to accomplish. Probes are equipped with many scientific instruments, like cameras and radiation detectors. Information from these instruments is radioed back to ground controllers on Earth.

ROSCOSMOS (ROSCOSMOS STATE CORPORATION FOR SPACE ACTIVITIES)

A government agency in charge of space flight missions for the Russian Federation. Headquartered in Moscow, Russia, it was established on February 25, 1992. It was formerly known simply as the Soviet space agency, a program of the former Soviet Union.

ROVER

A robotic vehicle that is driven over rough terrain by remote control.

SOVIET UNION

A former country that included a union of Russia and several other communist republics. It was formed in 1922 and existed until 1991.

SPACE RACE

The Space Race was a competition between the United States and the former Soviet Union (much of which is today's Russia). It started in the mid-1950s and lasted until the early 1970s. By the mid-1960s, both countries had sent probes to Venus. Mars was the next goal.

ONLINE RESOURCES

Booklinks
NONFICTION NETWORK
FREE! ONLINE NONFICTION RESOURCES

To learn more about Mars landers, visit abdobooklinks.com. These links are routinely monitored and updated to provide the most current information available.

INDEX